Developing

Artist

Correlates with...
Piano Literature Book 1
Piano Adventures Level 3A-3B

T0086918

PIANO SIGHTREADING BOOK 1

LATE ELEMENTARY WITH A CLASSICAL TWIST

by Nancy and Randall Faber

_____ is sightreading this book.

(Your Name)

Production Coordinator: Jon Ophoff
Cover: Terpstra Design, San Francisco

ISBN 978-1-61677-237-6
Copyright © 2023 Dovetree Productions, Inc.
c/o FABER PIANO ADVENTURES, 3042 Creek Dr., Ann Arbor, MI 48108.
International Copyright Secured. All Rights Reserved. Printed in U.S.A.

ABOUT PIANO SIGHTREADING BOOK 1

Sightreading skill is a powerful asset for the elementary pianist. This decoding skill requires *repetition* within familiar and changing musical patterns.

The book offers carefully composed "classic style" variations taken from pieces in **The Developing Artist Piano Literature Book 1**. The Sightreading Book 1 can be paired with the Literature Book 1 or used as a free-standing sightreading volume on its own. Use at Level 3A-3B of Piano Adventures, or its equivalent.

HOW TO USE

This book is organized into "sightreading sets" of 6 exercises—for 6 days of practice. Play one exercise a day, completing one set per week.

Think **sightread—STRATEGY—success!** The word "strategy" is the essential link between "sightread" and "success." The strategy has 3 steps:

1. Begin with Tap-a-Rhythm at the top of the page. These two-hand tapping exercises prepare the **rhythm patterns** in the piece. Short forays into metric counting help develop the student's "rhythmic mind."

   Day 1 might be done at the lesson. For the Tap-a-Rhythm exercise, tap and count with the student the first time through to coach **metric counting**. The student can count solo for the repeat.

   Spot check a rhythm from that set at the next lesson.

2. Have the student take a moment to scan the music for the following:

   time signature and **key signature**

   starting position

   rhythm patterns

   melodic patterns

   dynamics

3. Coach the student to set a slow tempo with one free count-off measure. Tell the student to keep going no matter what! Their skill at sightreading will grow and grow.

CHART YOUR PROGRESS

The student may circle each day when completed.

Sightreading for Piano Lit Book 1, pp. 4-5
Canario (Von der Hofe) 4-11

DAY 1   DAY 2   DAY 3   DAY 4   DAY 5   DAY 6

Sightreading for Piano Lit Book 1, pp. 6-7
Gavotte in C (Telemann) 12-19

DAY 1   DAY 2   DAY 3   DAY 4   DAY 5   DAY 6

Sightreading for Piano Lit Book 1, pp. 10-11
Bagatelle (Hook) 20-27

DAY 1   DAY 2   DAY 3   DAY 4   DAY 5   DAY 6

Sightreading for Piano Lit Book 1, p. 12
Minuet (Hook) 28-33

DAY 1   DAY 2   DAY 3   DAY 4   DAY 5   DAY 6

Sightreading for Piano Lit Book 1, p. 13
Little Dance (Türk) 34-39

DAY 1   DAY 2   DAY 3   DAY 4   DAY 5   DAY 6

Sightreading for Piano Lit Book 1, p. 14
Morning (Diabelli) 40-45

DAY 1   DAY 2   DAY 3   DAY 4   DAY 5   DAY 6

Sightreading for Piano Lit Book 1, p. 15
Quadrille (Haydn) 46-51

DAY 1   DAY 2   DAY 3   DAY 4   DAY 5   DAY 6

Sightreading for Piano Lit Book 1, pp. 16-17
Sontina in G, 1st Mvt. (Attwood) 52-61

DAY 1   DAY 2   DAY 3   DAY 4   DAY 5   DAY 6

Sightreading for Piano Lit Book 1, pp. 20-21
Little Prelude (Schytte) 62-69

DAY 1   DAY 2   DAY 3   DAY 4   DAY 5   DAY 6

Sightreading for Piano Lit Book 1, p. 22
Melody for Left Hand (Schytte)....... 70-75

DAY 1   DAY 2   DAY 3   DAY 4   DAY 5   DAY 6

Sightreading for Piano Lit Book 1, p. 23
Two Preludes (Spindler) 76-81

DAY 1   DAY 2   DAY 3   DAY 4   DAY 5   DAY 6

Sightreading for Piano Lit Book 1, pp. 28-29
Tarantella (Lynes) 82-89

DAY 1   DAY 2   DAY 3   DAY 4   DAY 5   DAY 6

Sightreading for Piano Lit Book 1, p. 34
Shepherd Pipes (Salutrinskaya) 90-95

DAY 1   DAY 2   DAY 3   DAY 4   DAY 5   DAY 6

CERTIFICATE 96

4

Tap-a-Rhythm: Tap and count aloud.

SIGHTREAD THE CLASSICS

Sightreading #1

Canario*

Joachim Von der Hofe
Variation, Faber

Allegretto

* from Piano Literature Book 1, pp. 4-5

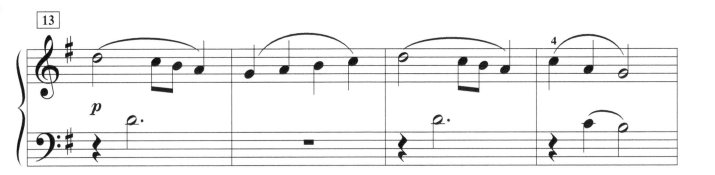

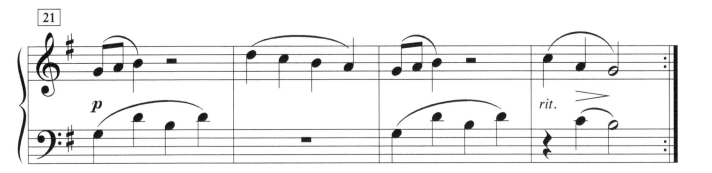

6

Tap-a-Rhythm: Tap and count aloud.

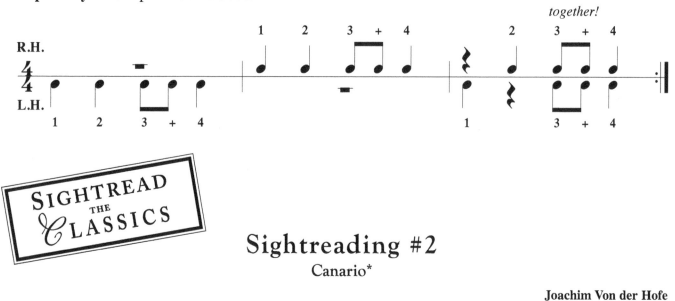

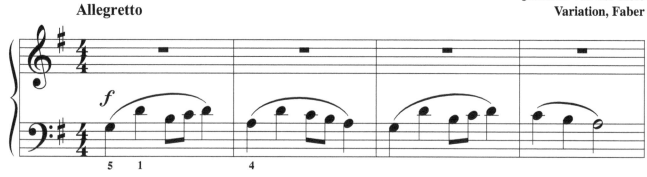

Sightreading #2
Canario*

Joachim Von der Hofe
Variation, Faber

Allegretto

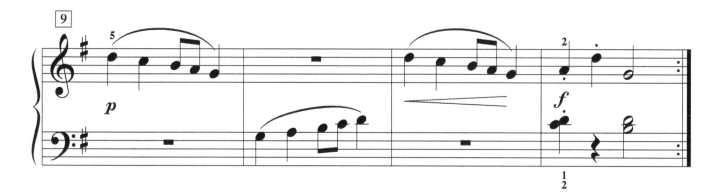

* from Piano Literature Book 1, pp. 4-5

Tap-a-Rhythm: Tap and count aloud.

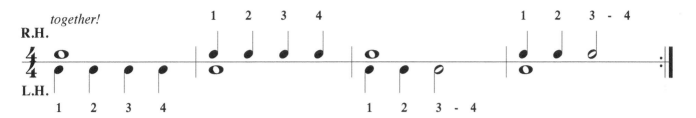

Sightreading #3
Canario*

Joachim Von der Hofe
Variation, Faber

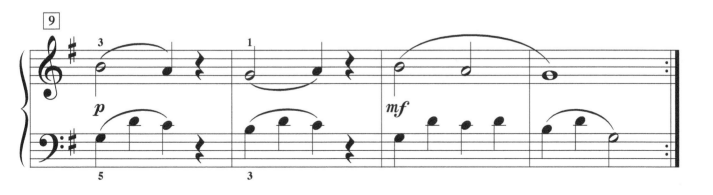

* from Piano Literature Book 1, pp. 4-5

Tap-a-Rhythm: Tap and count aloud.

SIGHTREAD THE CLASSICS

Sightreading #4
Canario
(for L.H. alone)*

Joachim Von der Hofe
Variation, Faber

Allegretto

* from Piano Literature Book 1, pp. 4-5

Tap-a-Rhythm: Tap and count aloud.

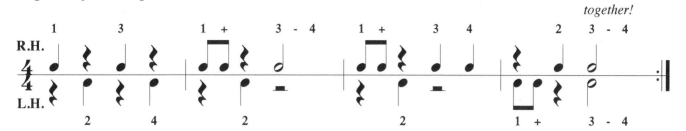

Sightreading #5

Canario*

Joachim Von der Hofe
Variation, Faber

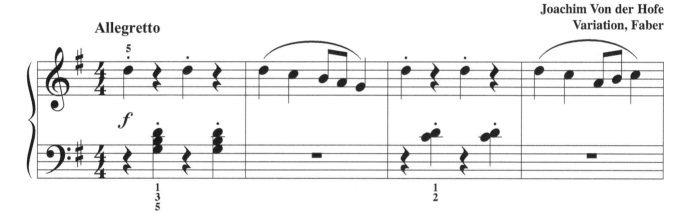

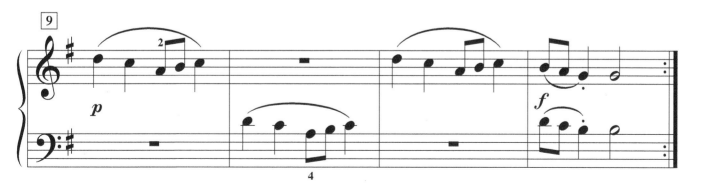

* from Piano Literature Book 1, pp. 4-5

Tap-a-Rhythm: Tap and count aloud.

SIGHTREAD
THE
CLASSICS

Sightreading #6
Canario*

Joachim Von der Hofe
Variation, Faber

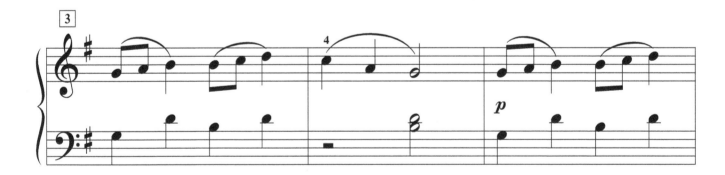

* from Piano Literature Book 1, pp. 4-5

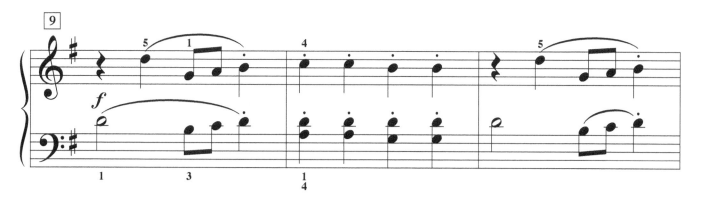

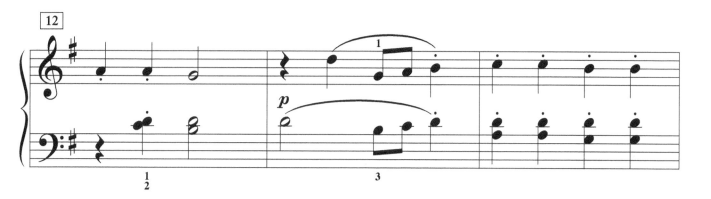

Tap-a-Rhythm: Tap and count aloud. Notice the two pick-up notes.

Sightreading #1
Gavotte in C*

Georg Philipp Telemann
Variation, Faber

* from Piano Literature Book 1, pp. 6-7

13

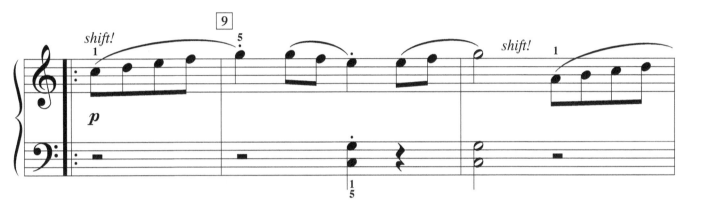

FF3059

Tap-a-Rhythm: Tap and count aloud. Notice the two beats of pick-up notes.

Sightreading #2
Gavotte in C*

Georg Philipp Telemann
Variation, Faber

* from Piano Literature Book 1, pp. 6-7

Sightreading #3

Gavotte in C*

Georg Philipp Telemann
Variation, Faber

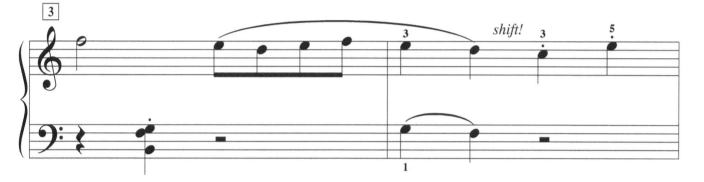

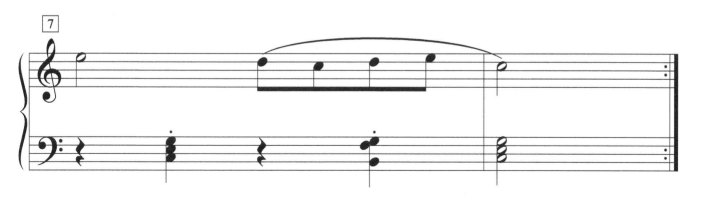

* from Piano Literature Book 1, pp. 6-7

Tap-a-Rhythm: Tap and count aloud. Notice the two pick-up notes.

Sightreading #4

Gavotte in C*
(for L.H. alone)

Georg Philipp Telemann
Variation, Faber

* from Piano Literature Book 1, pp. 6-7

Sightreading #5

Gavotte in C*

Georg Philipp Telemann
Variation, Faber

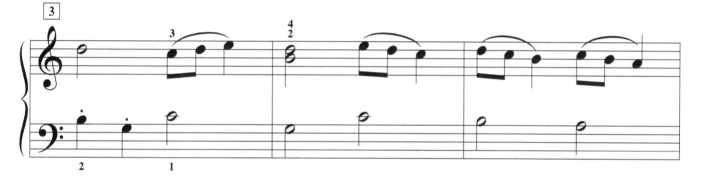

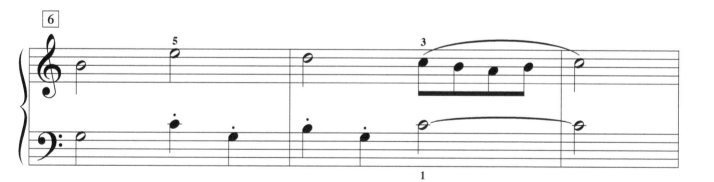

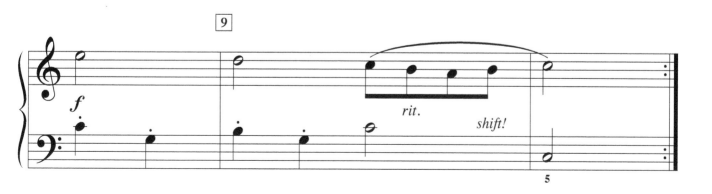

rit. *shift!*

* from Piano Literature Book 1, pp. 6-7

FF3059

Tap-a-Rhythm: Tap and count aloud. Notice the two beats of pick-up notes.

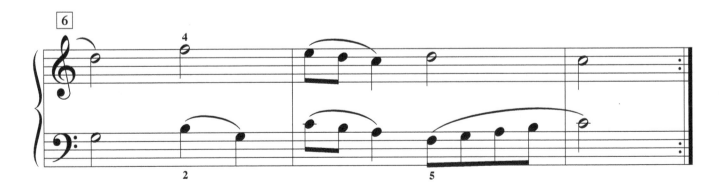

Sightreading #6

Gavotte in C*

Georg Philipp Telemann
Variation, Faber

* from Piano Literature Book 1, pp. 6-7

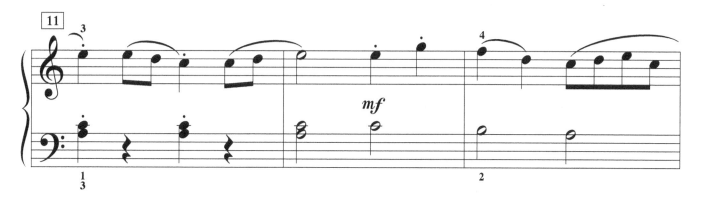

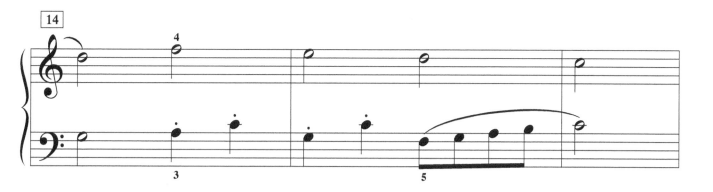

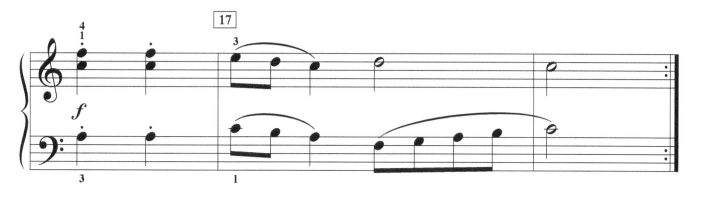

Tap-a-Rhythm: Tap and count aloud.

Sightreading #1
Bagatelle*

James Hook
Variation, Faber

Allegro

*from Piano Literature Book 1, pp. 10-11

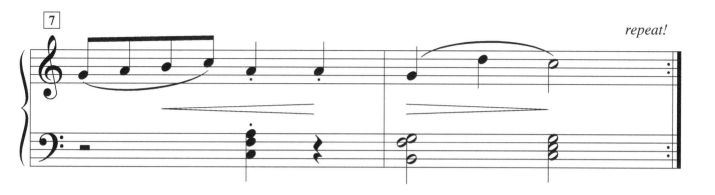

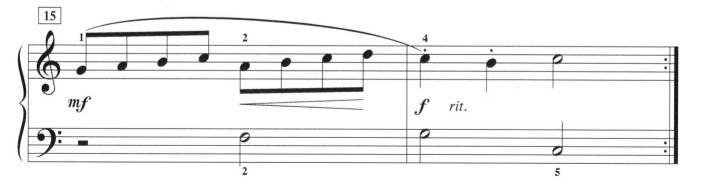

Tap-a-Rhythm: Tap and count aloud.

SIGHTREAD THE CLASSICS

Sightreading #2
Bagatelle*

James Hook
Variation, Faber

* from Piano Literature Book 1, pp. 10-11

Sightreading #3

Bagatelle*

James Hook
Variation, Faber

* from Piano Literature Book 1, pp. 10-11

FF3059

Tap-a-Rhythm: Tap and count aloud.

SIGHTREAD
THE
CLASSICS

Sightreading #4
Bagatelle*
(for L.H. alone)

James Hook
Variation, Faber

* from Piano Literature Book 1, pp. 10-11

Sightreading #5

Bagatelle*

James Hook
Variation, Faber

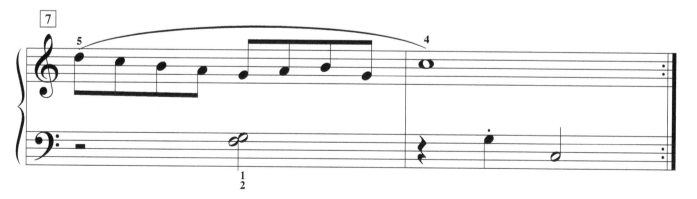

* from Piano Literature Book 1, pp. 10-11

Tap-a-Rhythm: Tap and count aloud.

SIGHTREAD THE **CLASSICS**

Sightreading #6
Bagatelle*

James Hook
Variation, Faber

Allegro

f

p

* from Piano Literature Book 1, pp. 10-11

repeat!

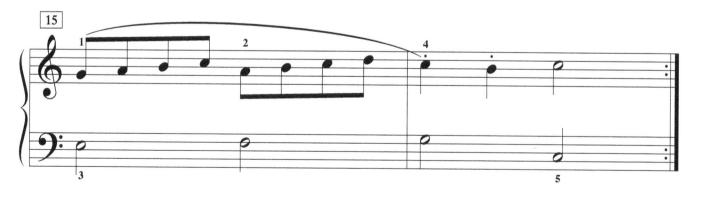

28

Tap-a-Rhythm: Tap and count aloud.

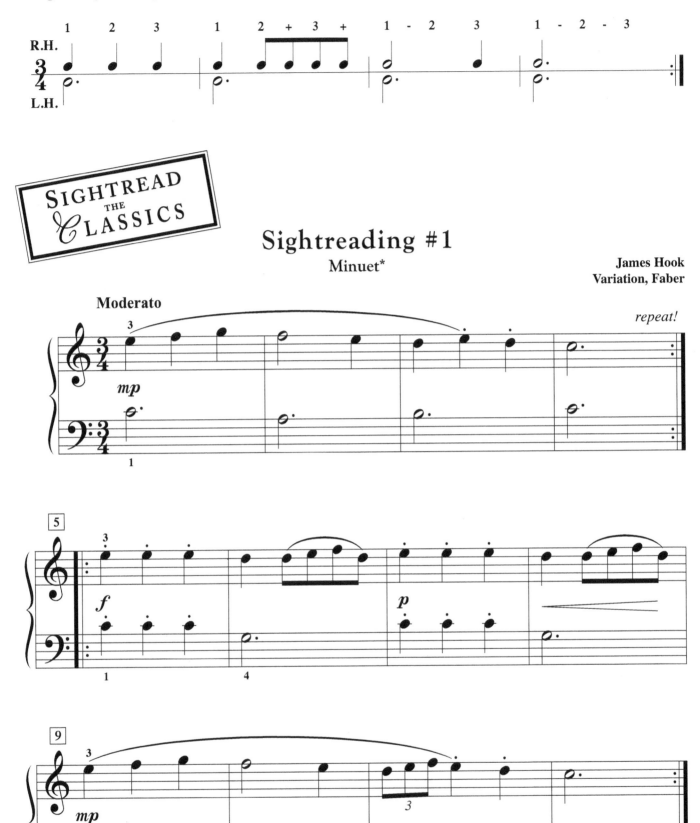

Sightreading #1
Minuet*

James Hook
Variation, Faber

Moderato

repeat!

mp

f

p

mp

* from Piano Literature Book 1, p. 12

Sightreading #2

Minuet*

James Hook
Variation, Faber

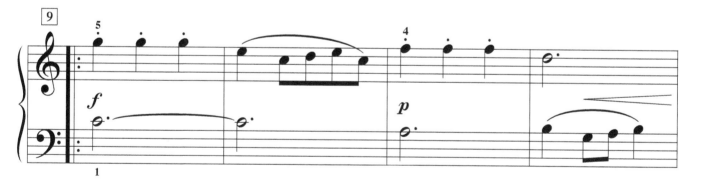

* from Piano Literature Book 1, p. 12

Tap-a-Rhythm: Tap and count aloud.

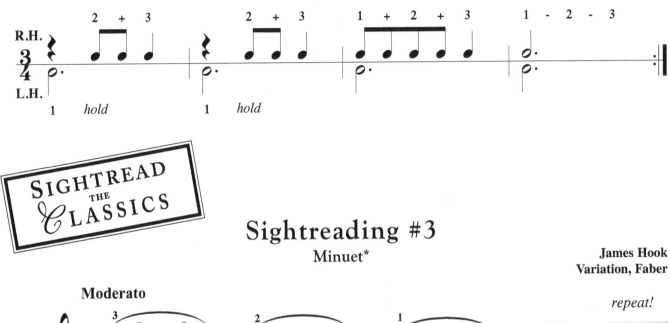

Sightreading #3
Minuet*

James Hook
Variation, Faber

* from Piano Literature Book 1, p. 12

Sightreading #4

Minuet*

(for L.H. alone)

James Hook
Variation, Faber

Moderato

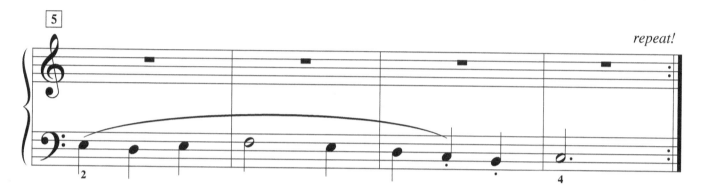

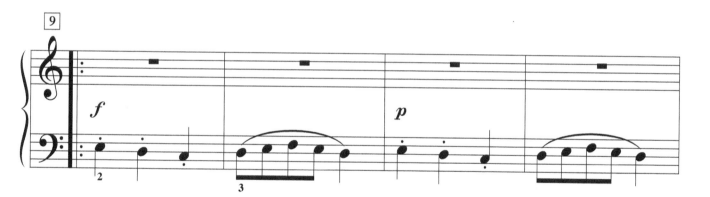

* from Piano Literature Book 1, p. 12

FF3059

Tap-a-Rhythm: Tap and count aloud.

SIGHTREAD THE CLASSICS

Sightreading #5
Minuet*

James Hook
Variation, Faber

repeat!

Moderato

mp

f

mp

* from Piano Literature Book 1, p. 12

Sightreading #6
Minuet*

James Hook
Variation, Faber

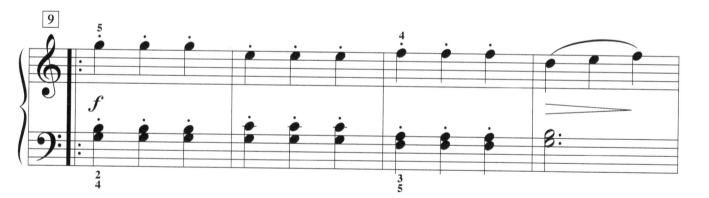

* from Piano Literature Book 1, p. 12

Tap-a-Rhythm: Tap and count aloud.

Sightreading #1

Little Dance*

Daniel Gottlob Türk
Variation, Faber

* from Piano Literature Book 1, p. 13

Sightreading #2

Little Dance*

Daniel Gottlob Türk
Variation, Faber

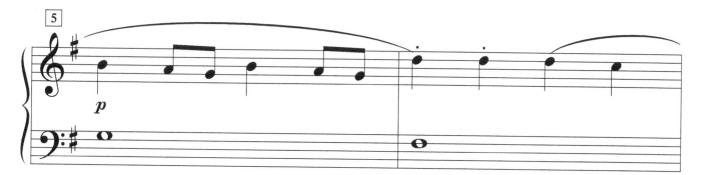

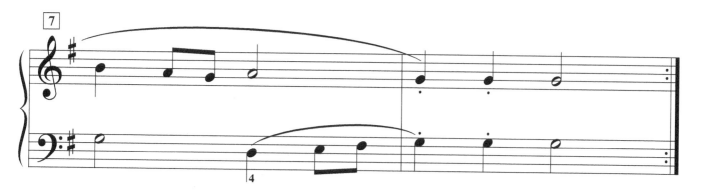

* from Piano Literature Book 1, p. 13

Tap-a-Rhythm: Tap and count aloud.

Sightreading #3
Little Dance*

Daniel Gottlob Türk
Variation, Faber

Allegretto

* from Piano Literature Book 1, p. 13

Sightreading #4
Little Dance*

Daniel Gottlob Türk
Variation, Faber

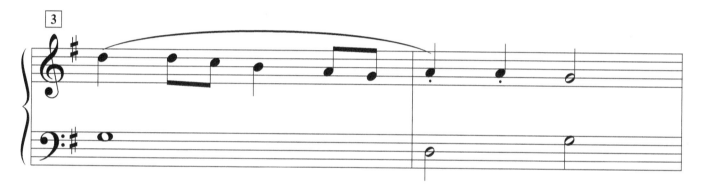

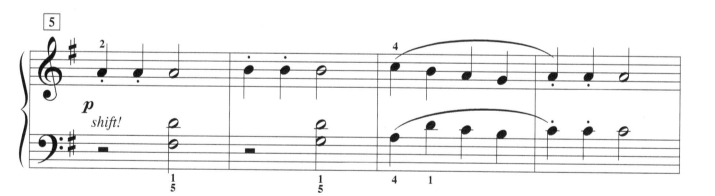

* from Piano Literature Book 1, p. 13

Tap-a-Rhythm: Tap and count aloud.

Sightreading #5

Little Dance*
(for L.H. alone)

Daniel Gottlob Türk
Variation, Faber

* from Piano Literature Book 1, p. 13

Sightreading #6
Little Dance*

Daniel Gottlob Türk
Variation, Faber

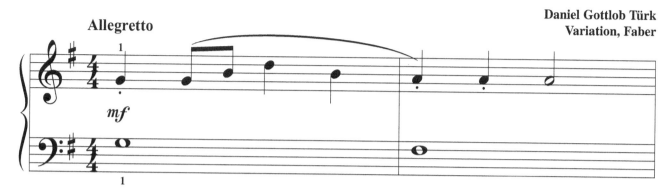

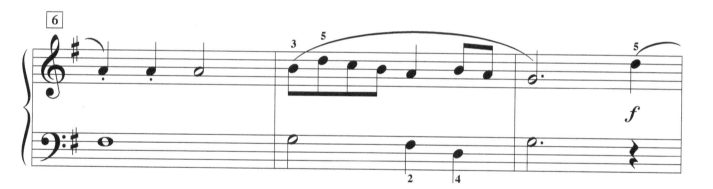

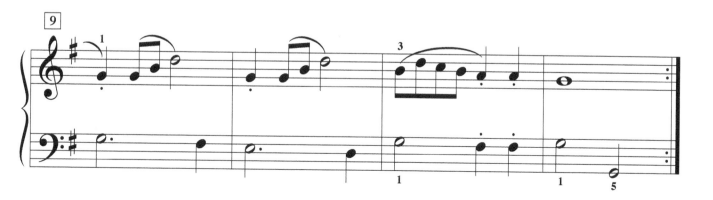

* from Piano Literature Book 1, p. 13

40

Tap-a-Rhythm: Tap and count aloud.

Sightreading #1
Morning*

Anton Diabelli
Variation, Faber

* from Piano Literature Book 1, p. 14

Sightreading #2
Morning*

Anton Diabelli
Variation, Faber

* from Piano Literature Book 1, p. 14

Tap-a-Rhythm: Tap and count aloud.

Sightreading #3
Morning*

Anton Diabelli
Variation, Faber

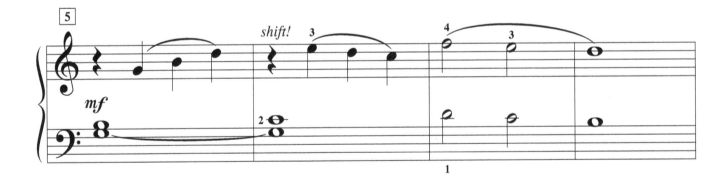

* from Piano Literature Book 1, p. 14

Sightreading #4

Morning*

Anton Diabelli
Variation, Faber

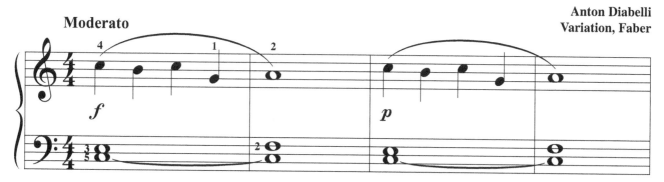

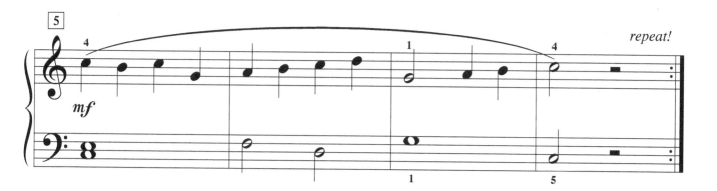

* from Piano Literature Book 1, p. 14

FF3059

Tap-a-Rhythm: Tap and count aloud.

Sightreading #5
Morning*

Anton Diabelli
Variation, Faber

Moderato

* from Piano Literature Book 1, p. 14

Sightreading #6

Morning*
(for L.H. alone)

Anton Diabelli
Variation, Faber

Moderato

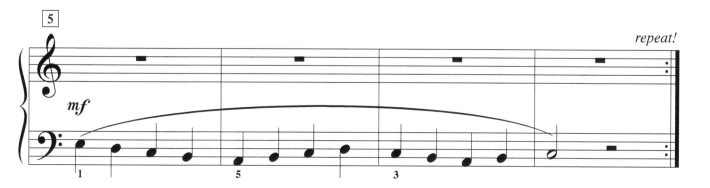

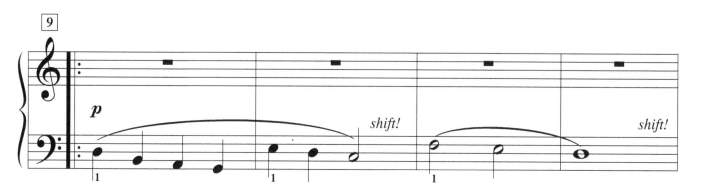

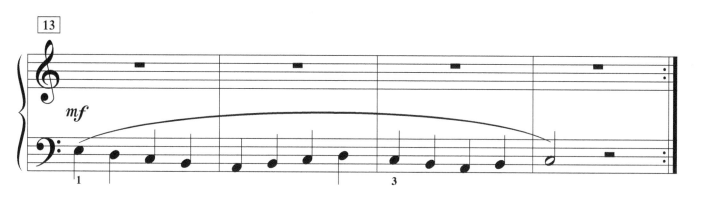

* from Piano Literature Book 1, p. 14

FF3059

Tap-a-Rhythm: Tap and count aloud. Notice the pick-up note.

Sightreading #1
Quadrille*

Franz Joseph Haydn
Variation, Faber

Allegretto

* from Piano Literature Book 1, p. 15

Sightreading #2

Quadrille*

Franz Joseph Haydn
Variation, Faber

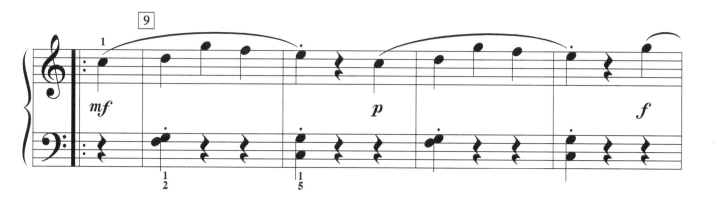

* from Piano Literature Book 1, p. 15

48

Sightreading #3

Quadrille*

Franz Joseph Haydn
Variation, Faber

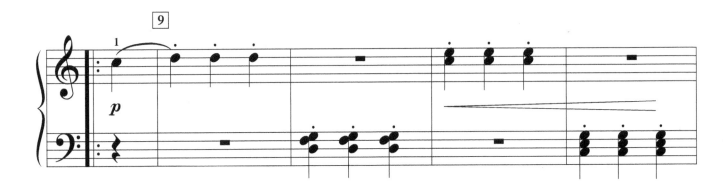

* from Piano Literature Book 1, p. 15

Sightreading #4

Quadrille*

Franz Joseph Haydn
Variation, Faber

Allegretto

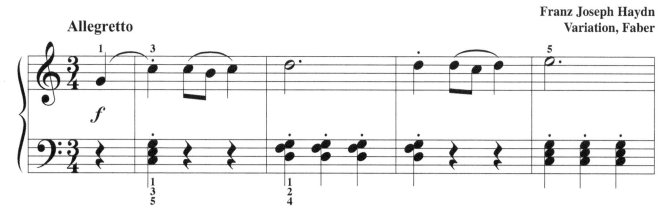

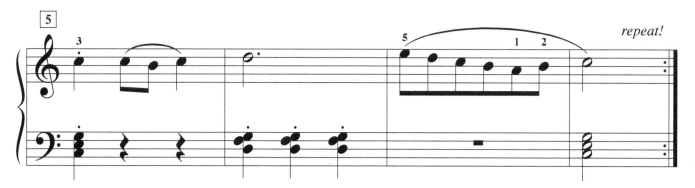

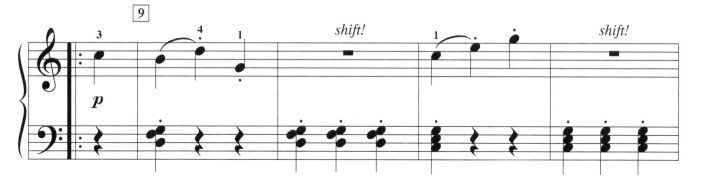

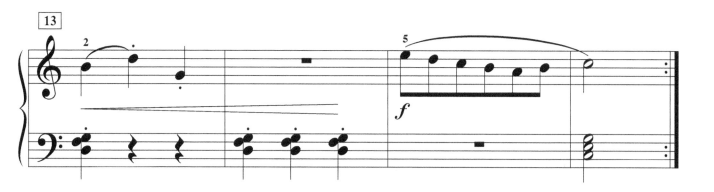

* from Piano Literature Book 1, p. 15

FF3059

50

Tap-a-Rhythm: Tap and count aloud. Notice the pick-up note.

Sightreading #5

Quadrille*

(L.H. alone)

Franz Joseph Haydn
Variation, Faber

Allegretto

* from Piano Literature Book 1, p. 15

Sightreading #6
Quadrille*

Franz Joseph Haydn
Variation, Faber

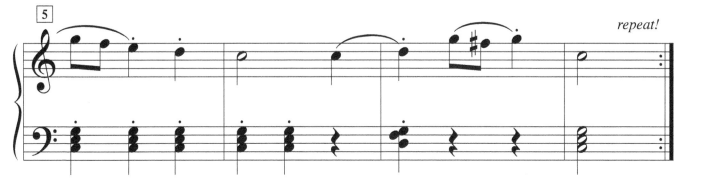

* from Piano Literature Book 1, p. 15

Tap-a-Rhythm: Tap and count aloud. Notice the pick-up note.

Sightreading #1
Sontina in G, 1st Movement*

Thomas Attwood
Variation, Faber

Allegretto

* from Piano Literature Book 1, pp. 16-17

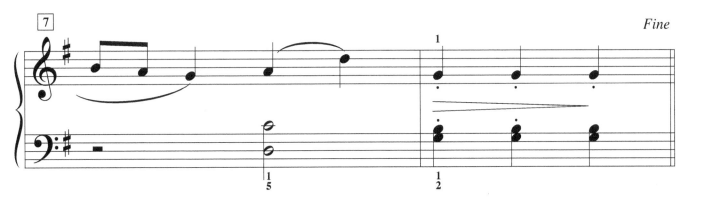

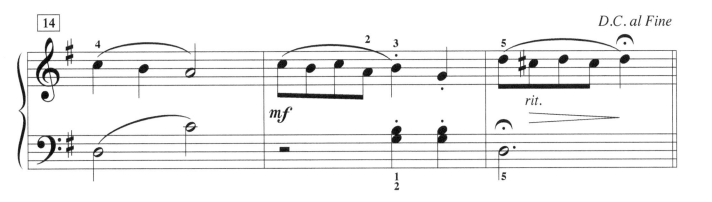

Sightreading #2

Sontina in G, 1st Movement*

Thomas Attwood
Variation, Faber

Allegretto

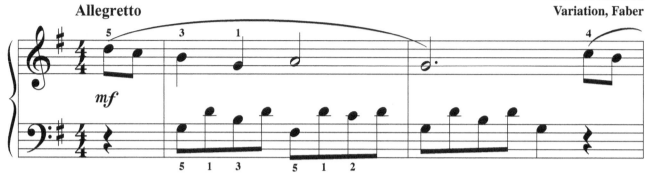

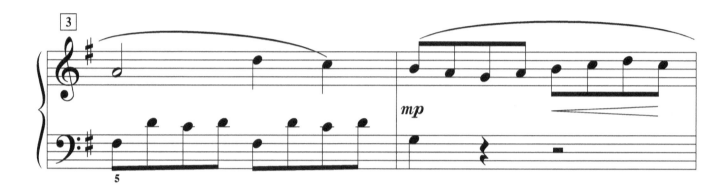

* from Piano Literature Book 1, pp. 16-17

Sightreading #3

Sontina in G, 1st Movement*

Thomas Attwood
Variation, Faber

Allegretto

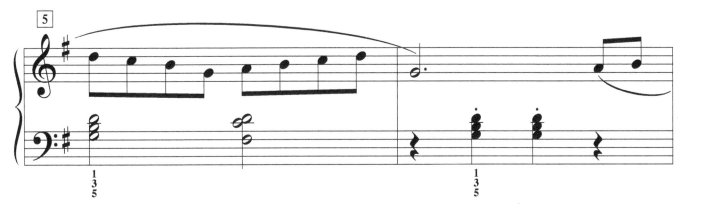

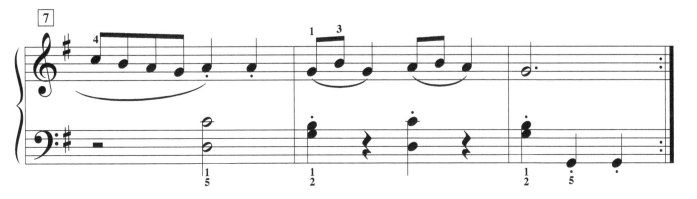

* from Piano Literature Book 1, pp. 16-17

Sightreading #4

Sontina in G, 1st Movement*

Thomas Attwood
Variation, Faber

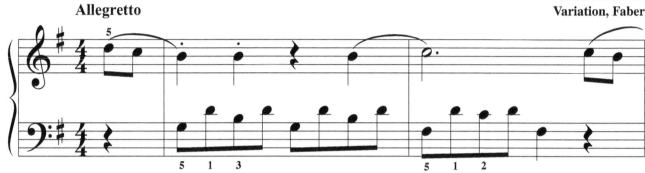

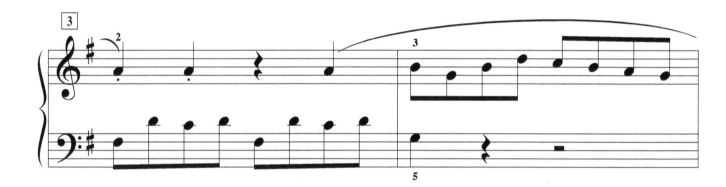

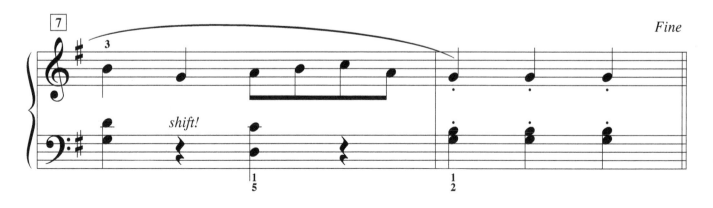

* from Piano Literature Book 1, pp. 16-17

FF3059

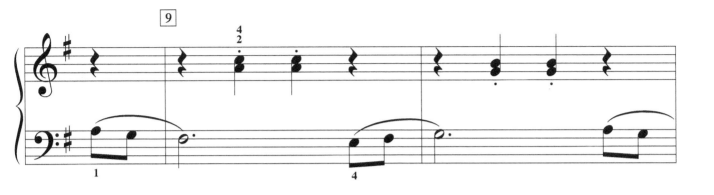

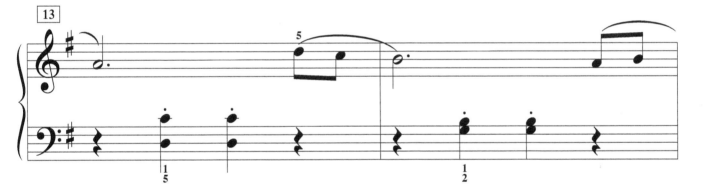

Sightreading #5

Sontina in G, 1st Movement*

Thomas Attwood
Variation, Faber

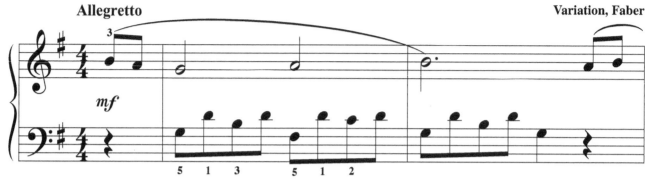

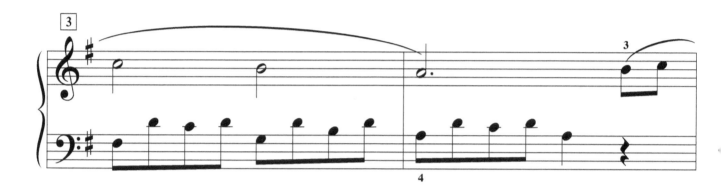

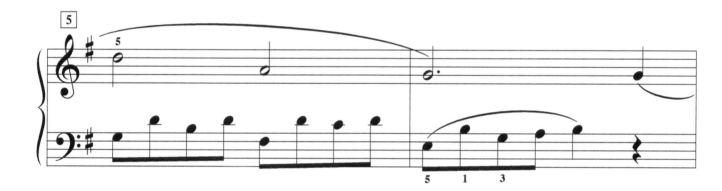

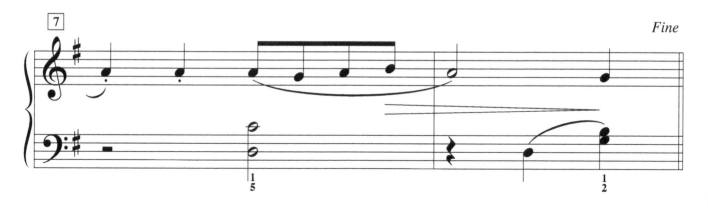

* from Piano Literature Book 1, pp. 16-17

FF3059

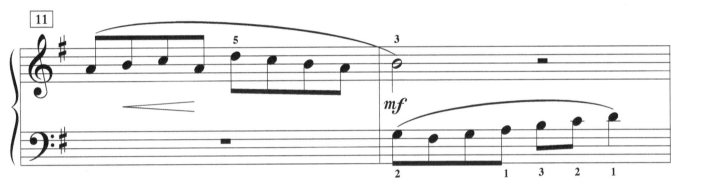

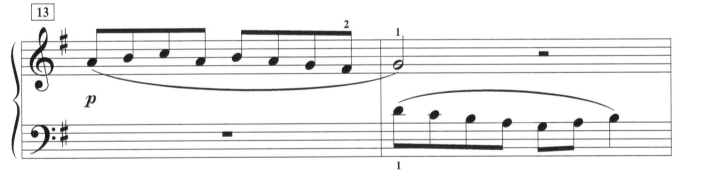

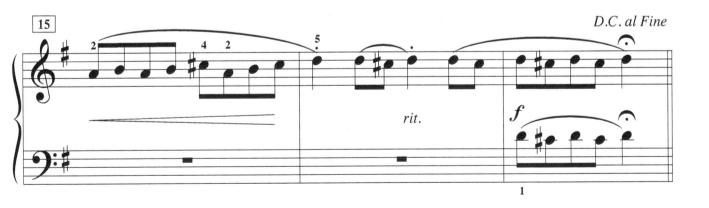

Tap-a-Rhythm: Tap and count aloud. Notice the pick-up notes.

Sightreading #6
Sontina in G, 1st Movement*

Thomas Attwood
Variation, Faber

Allegretto

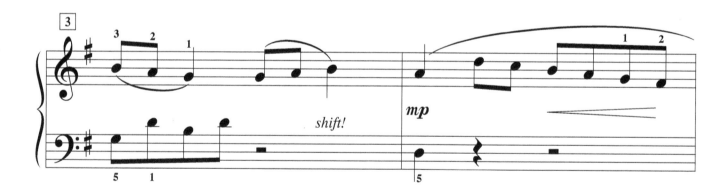

* from Piano Literature Book 1, pp. 16-17

FF3059

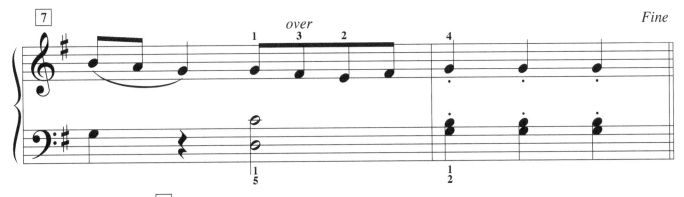

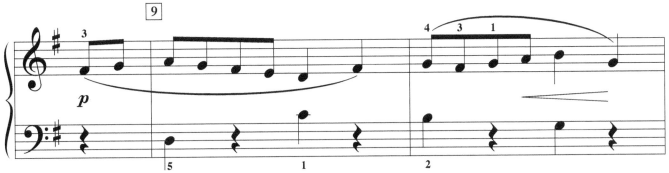

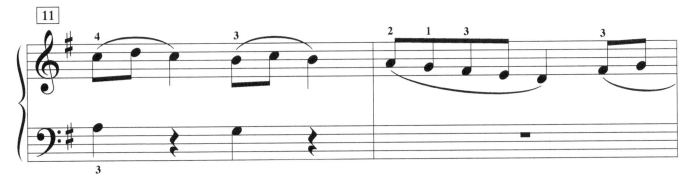

Tap-a-Rhythm: Tap and count aloud.

Sightreading #1

Little Prelude*

Ludwig Schytte
Variation, Faber

Moderato

* from Piano Literature Book 1, pp. 20-21

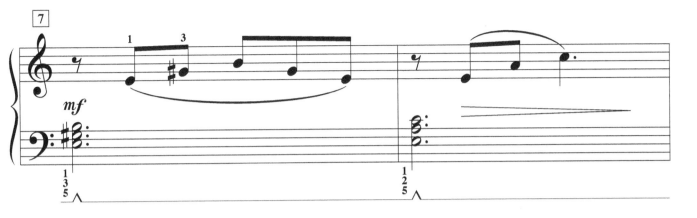

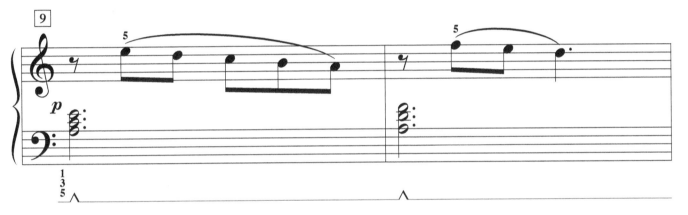

SIGHTREAD THE **CLASSICS**

Sightreading #2
Little Prelude*

Ludwig Schytte
Variation, Faber

Moderato

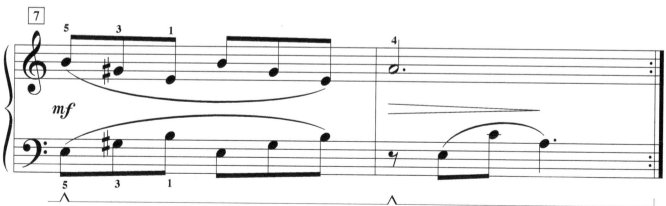

* from Piano Literature Book 1, pp. 20-21

Sightreading #3

Little Prelude*

Ludwig Schytte
Variation, Faber

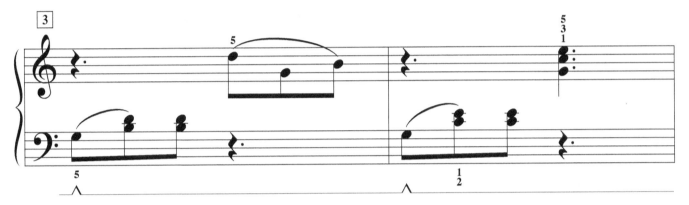

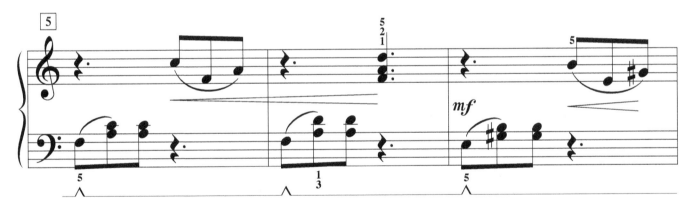

* from Piano Literature Book 1, pp. 20-21

FF3059

Tap-a-Rhythm: Tap and count aloud.

Sightreading #4
Little Prelude*

Ludwig Schytte
Variation, Faber

* from Piano Literature Book 1, pp. 20-21

Sightreading #5

Little Prelude*

Ludwig Schytte
Variation, Faber

* from Piano Literature Book 1, pp. 20-21

Tap-a-Rhythm: Tap and count aloud.

Sightreading #6
Little Prelude*

Ludwig Schytte
Variation, Faber

* from Piano Literature Book 1, pp. 20-21

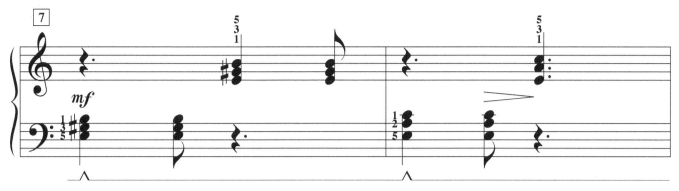

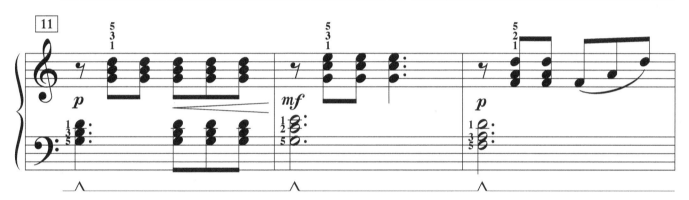

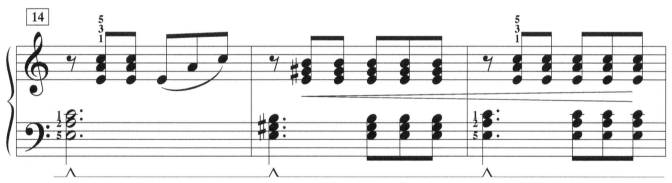

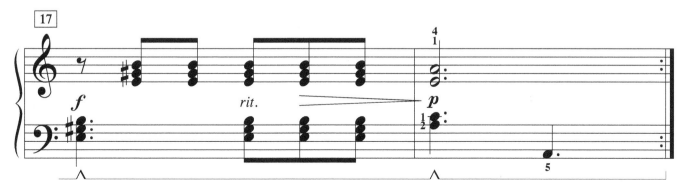

FF3059

Tap-a-Rhythm: Tap and count aloud.

SIGHTREAD THE CLASSICS

Sightreading #1
Melody for Left Hand*

Ludwig Schytte
Variation, Faber

Moderato

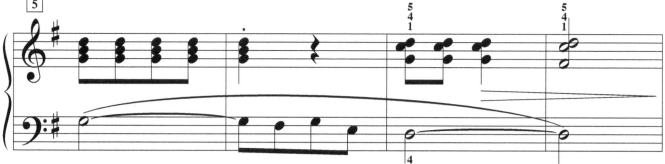

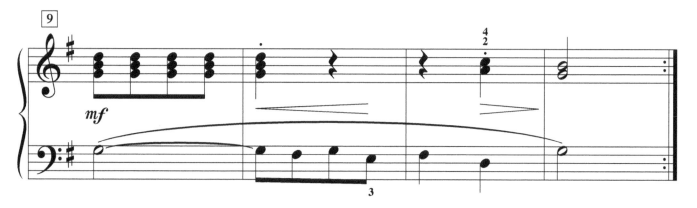

* from Piano Literature Book 1, p. 22

Sightreading #2

Melody for Left Hand*

Ludwig Schytte
Variation, Faber

Moderato

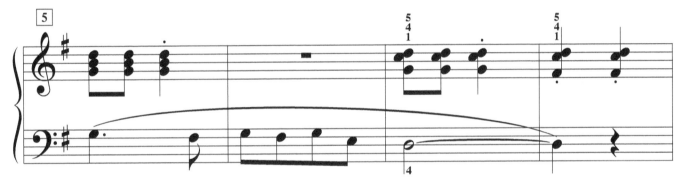

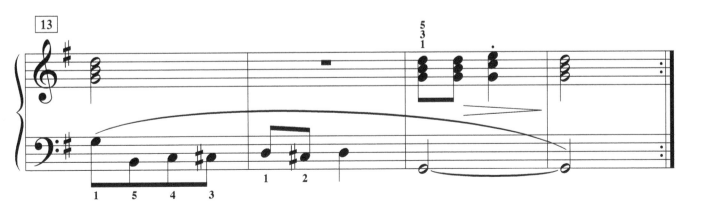

* from Piano Literature Book 1, p. 22

Tap-a-Rhythm: Tap and count aloud.

Sightreading #3
Melody for Left Hand*

Ludwig Schytte
Variation, Faber

Moderato

* from Piano Literature Book 1, p. 22

Sightreading #4
Melody for Left Hand*

Ludwig Schytte
Variation, Faber

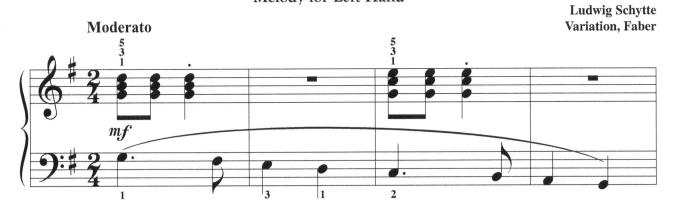

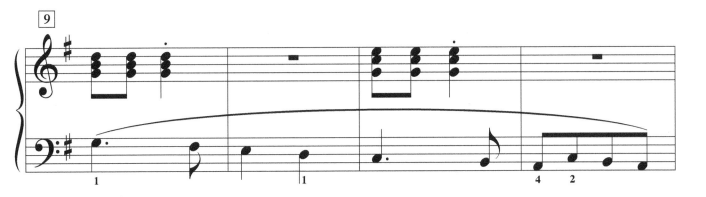

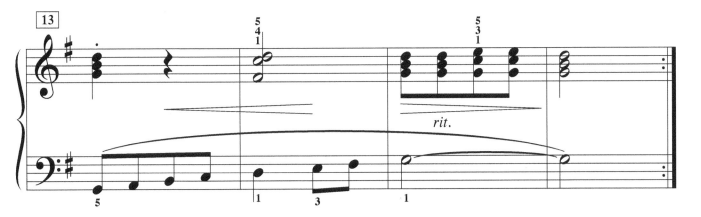

* from Piano Literature Book 1, p. 22

74

Tap-a-Rhythm: Tap and count aloud.

Sightreading #5
Melody for Left Hand*
(L.H. alone)

Ludwig Schytte
Variation, Faber

Moderato

* from Piano Literature Book 1, p. 22

Sightreading #6

Melody for Left Hand*

Ludwig Schytte
Variation, Faber

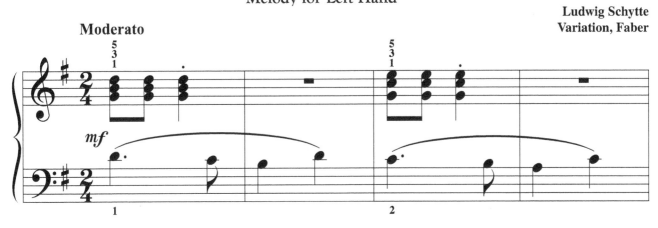

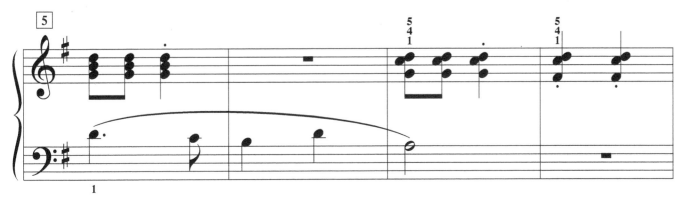

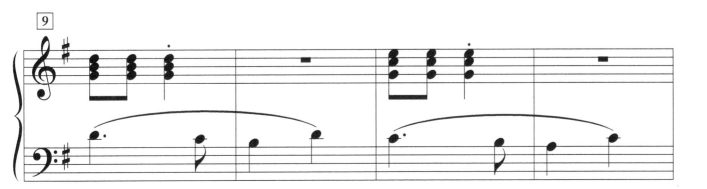

* from Piano Literature Book 1, p. 22

Tap-a-Rhythm: Tap and count aloud.

Sightreading #1

Prelude I*

Fritz Spindler
Variation, Faber

* from Piano Literature Book 1, p. 23

Tap-a-Rhythm: Tap and count aloud.

Sightreading #2
Prelude II*

Fritz Spindler
Variation, Faber

* from Piano Literature Book 1, p. 23

Tap-a-Rhythm: Tap and count aloud.

Sightreading #3
Prelude I*

Fritz Spindler
Variation, Faber

Tap-a-Rhythm: Tap and count aloud.

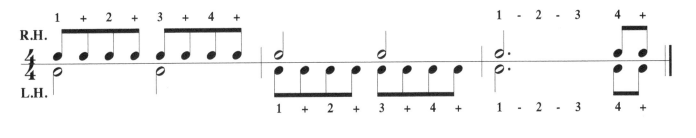

Sightreading #4
Prelude II*

Fritz Spindler
Variation, Faber

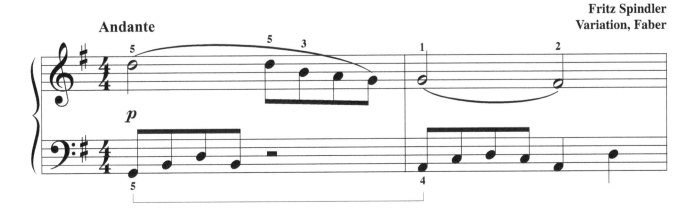

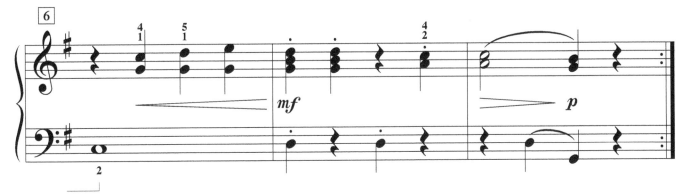

* from Piano Literature Book 1, p. 23

Sightreading #5

Prelude I*

Fritz Spindler
Variation, Faber

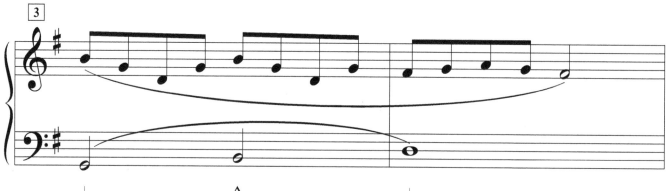

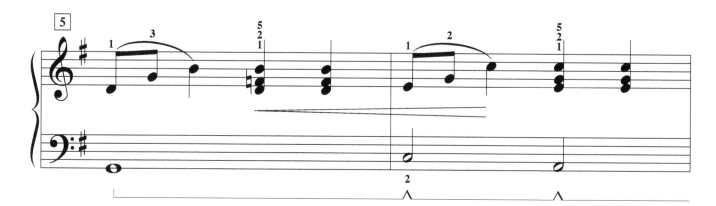

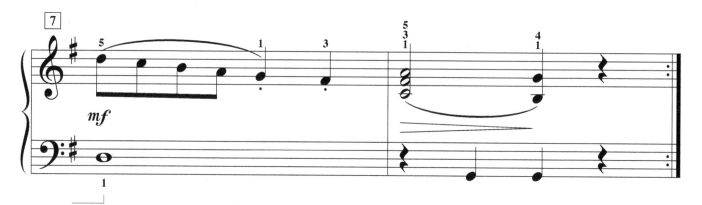

* from Piano Literature Book 1, p. 23

Sightreading #6
Prelude II*

Fritz Spindler
Variation, Faber

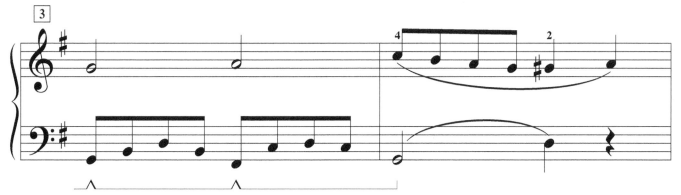

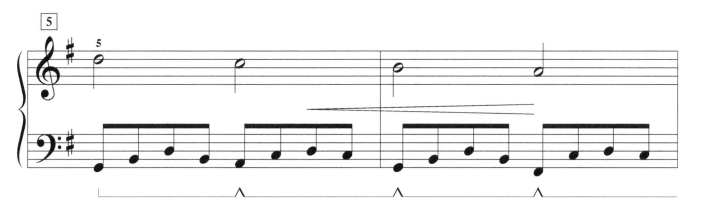

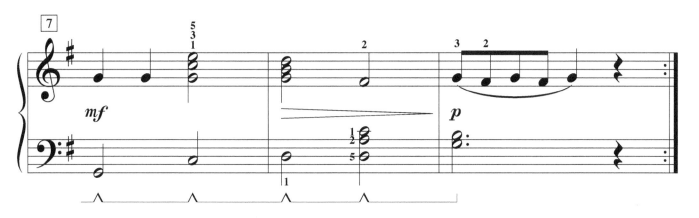

* from Piano Literature Book 1, p. 23

Tap-a-Rhythm: Tap and count aloud. Notice the pick-up note.

Sightreading #1

Tarantella*

Frank Lynes
Variation, Faber

Allegro

* from Piano Literature Book 1, pp. 28-29

Sightreading #2
Tarantella*

Frank Lynes
Variation, Faber

Allegro

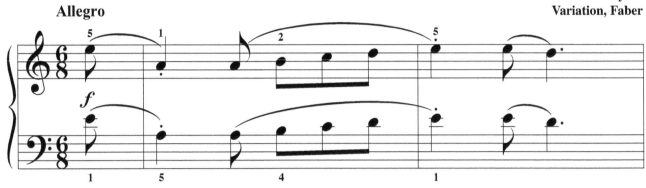

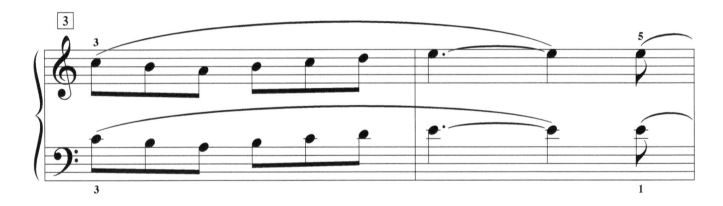

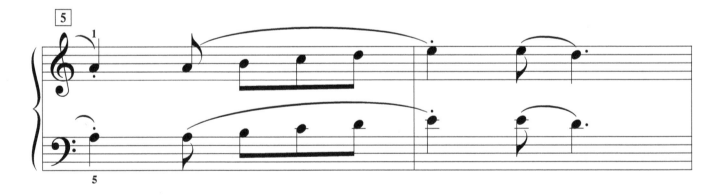

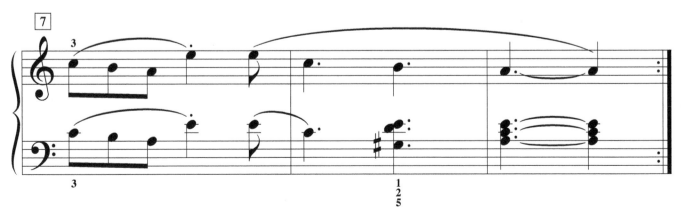

* from Piano Literature Book 1, pp. 28-29

FF3059

Sightreading #3
Tarantella*

Frank Lynes
Variation, Faber

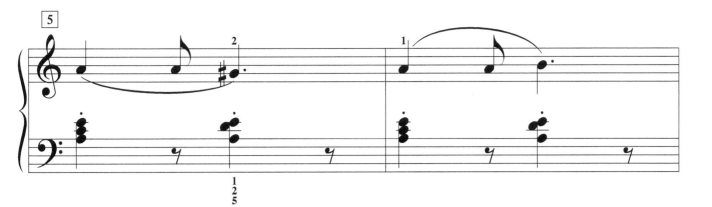

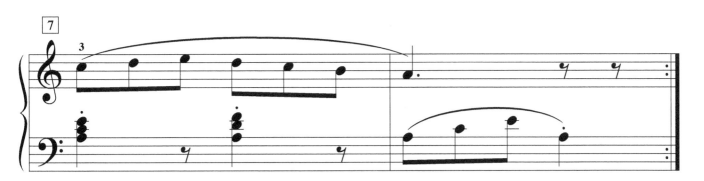

* from Piano Literature Book 1, pp. 28-29

Sightreading #4
Tarantella*

Frank Lynes
Variation, Faber

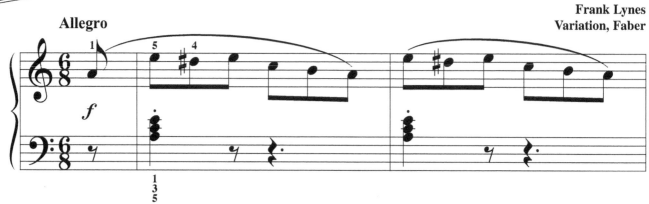

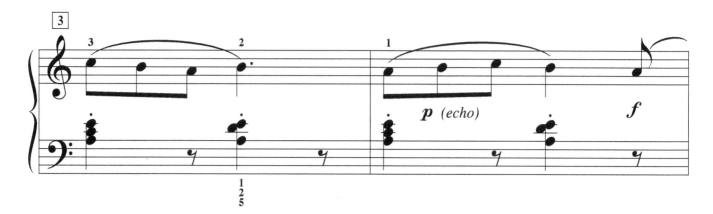

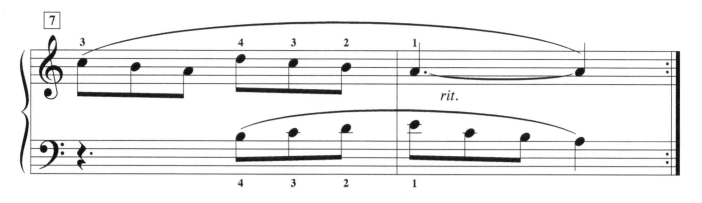

* from Piano Literature Book 1, pp. 28-29

FF3059

Sightreading #5

Tarantella*

Frank Lynes
Variation, Faber

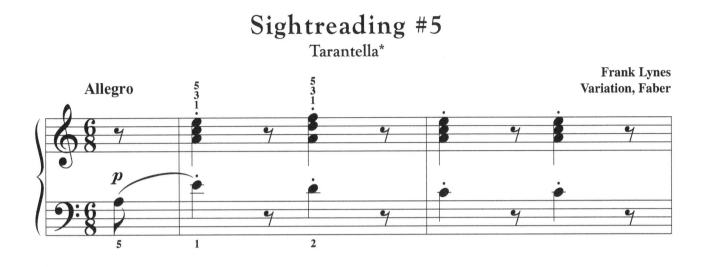

* from Piano Literature Book 1, pp. 28-29

Tap-a-Rhythm: Tap and count aloud. Notice the pick-up note.

Sightreading #6

*Tarantella**

Frank Lynes
Variation, Faber

Allegro

* from Piano Literature Book 1, pp. 28-29

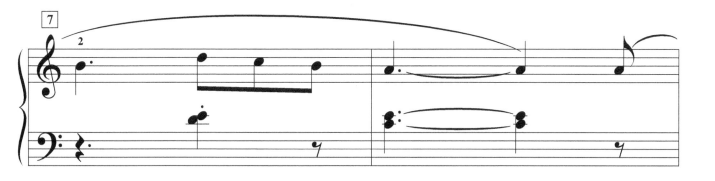

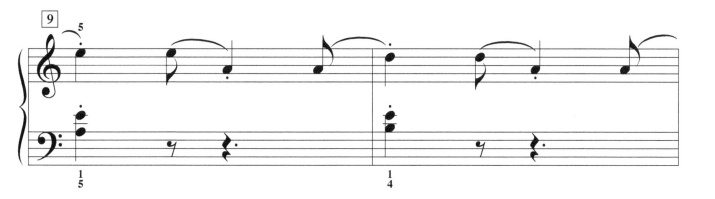

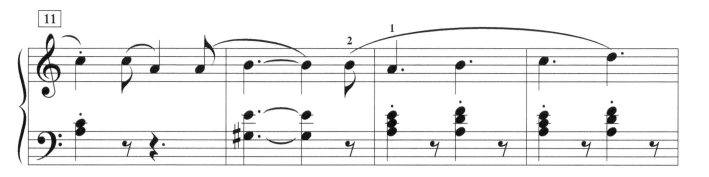

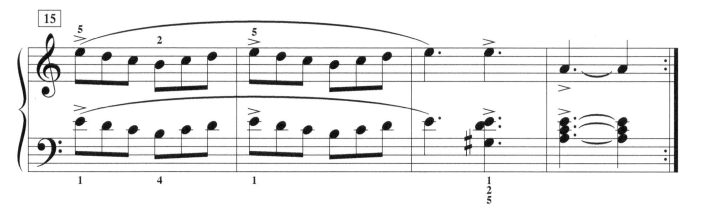

Tap-a-Rhythm: Tap and count aloud.

Sightreading #1
Shepherd Pipes*

Tat'iana Salutrinskaya
Variation, Faber

Gently

Sightreading #2
Shepherd Pipes*

Tat'iana Salutrinskaya
Variation, Faber

* from Piano Literature Book 1, p. 34

Tap-a-Rhythm: Tap and count aloud.

SIGHTREAD THE **CLASSICS**

Sightreading #3
Shepherd Pipes*
(for L.H. alone)

Tat'iana Salutrinskaya
Variation, Faber

Gently

* from Piano Literature Book 1, p. 34

FF3059

Sightreading #4
Shepherd Pipes*

Tat'iana Salutrinskaya
Variation, Faber

* from Piano Literature Book 1, p. 34

Sightreading #5
Shepherd Pipes*

Tat'iana Salutrinskaya
Variation, Faber

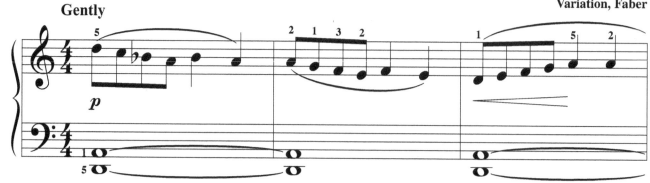

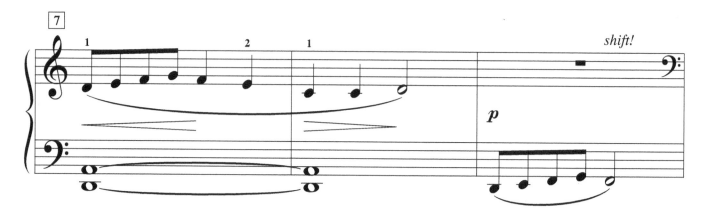

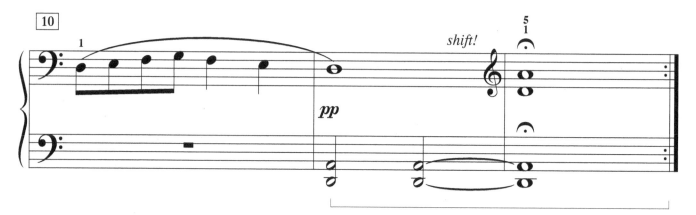

* from Piano Literature Book 1, p. 34

Sightreading #6

Shepherd Pipes*

Tat'iana Salutrinskaya
Variation, Faber

* from Piano Literature Book 1, p. 34

FF3059

Congratulations!

You have completed The Developing Artist
Piano Sightreading Book 1

CERTIFICATE OF ACHIEVEMENT

Student's Name

_____

Teacher's Name

_____

Completion Date

_____

You are now ready for
The Developing Artist Piano Literature BOOK 2
The Developing Artist Piano Sightreading BOOK 2